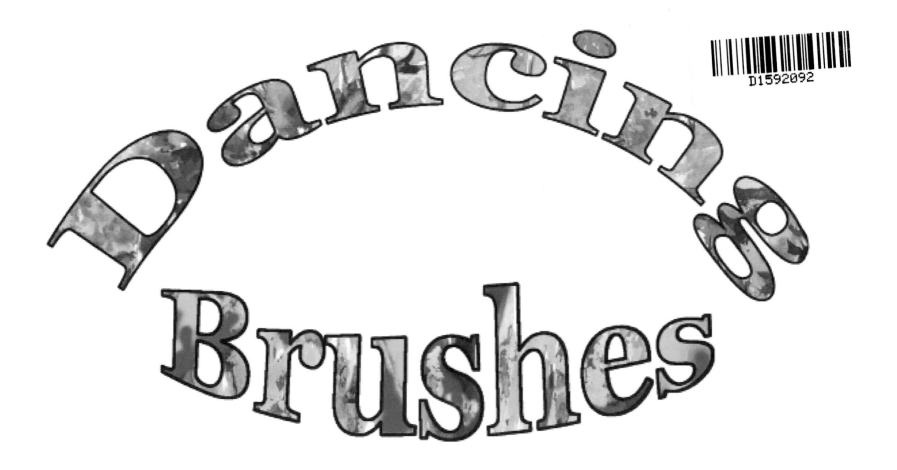

Dancing Brushes

**A Fresh Approach to
Watercolor**

With Rae Andrews

**Leaning Rock Press
Gales Ferry, CT**

Leaning Rock Press, LLC
Gales Ferry, CT 06335
leaningrockpress@gmail.com
www.leaningrockpress.com

978-1-950323-45-6, Hardcover
978-1-950323-47-0, Softcover

Library of Congress Control Number: 2021908581

Publisher's Cataloging-In-Publication Data
(Prepared by The Donohue Group, Inc.)
Names: Andrews, Rae, author.
Title: Dancing brushes : a watercolor journey / with Rae Andrews.
Description: Gales Ferry, CT : Leaning Rock Press, [2021]
Identifiers: ISBN 9781950323456 (hardcover) | ISBN 9781950323470 (softcover)
Subjects: LCSH: Watercolor painting--Technique. | Color in art. | Andrews, Rae--Catalogs.
Classification: LCC ND2420 .A54 2021 | DDC 751.422--dc23

Printed in the United States of America

Table of Contents

About Rae

Rae Andrews is an international art teacher with 50 years of teaching experience.

A native Australian from Sydney, Rae chose hairdressing as a career. However, she always painted and harbored a dream of becoming a full-time artist.

While simultaneously running several of her own hair salons, Rae began teaching art in the 1970s. In 1982, she sold all of her businesses to attend college full-time and achieve her art degree.

An entrepreneur at heart, she founded the Northside Art School in the Sydney suburb of Elanora. With the popularity of her teaching methods, the school flourished, and Rae added four more teachers.

Life changed when Rae met and married her American husband, Thomas, and they moved to the island of Maui, Hawaii.

During the next 12 years, Rae owned two art galleries on the island and traveled back and forth to Australia to teach workshops.

Home is now Austin, Texas, where Rae teaches online Zoom workshops and classes. She also travels and conducts workshops in Europe.

To see more of Rae's work, visit raeandrews.com.

Introduction

As a teacher of this wonderful medium over the last 50 years, I have had the great privilege of watching students grow in their own personal journeys. Many are rushing to adapt a style before they learn the basics, such as drawing and color mixing. I don't believe any new artist should be in such a rush to develop a style, per se. That will definitely come over time and practice.

Watercolor is such a spontaneous medium, we all know that, and it's full of surprises and sometimes messes, or 'stinkers' as I call them. I advise students to explore the many exciting properties, and find their own way, to keep that magical discovery alive.

This book is all about the different approaches used in my own paintings. I expect my readers to do some of their own color theory and compositional alternatives by drawing often and experimenting.

Not every demonstration here will resonate with every reader, however the many approaches and techniques I am showing, should certainly help with your own creative options.

I am a colorist and love design. Hence my paintings tend to have a different look for my viewers. I've discovered that color and a dramatic choice of value helps surprise the eye, and individualizes my work.

Finally, I hope you enjoy what I have features in the following pages, and feel inspired to strive and forge forward on your own path.
Dare to be different and above all, have fun!
Rae

A Sense of Drama

4

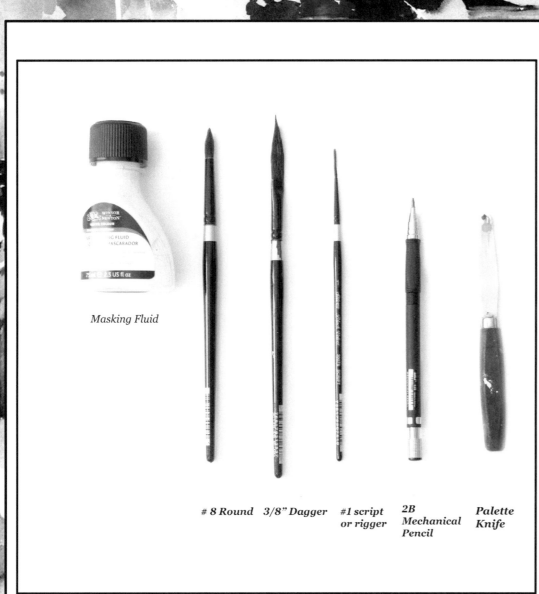

Masking Fluid

8 Round   3/8" Dagger   #1 script or rigger   2B Mechanical Pencil   Palette Knife

My Colors for this demonstration

I use Daniel Smith (DS) and Winsor and Newton (WN)
Lucas (L)
All Tube Colors

Lemon Yellow (DS)
Permanent Sap Green (WN)
Turquoise (L)
Cobalt Blue (DS)
French Ultramarine Blue (DS)

I use my palette knife on the very tip to get fine and slightly thicker lines, and some drips and splashes off the end of it for variation.

The first step for this painting is to disturb the surface tension with a few lines and splashes of masking fluid before drawing out my subject.

I allow a few splashes and drips to fall off my palette knife onto the surface before I dry.

Be aware of the negative spaces. They need to be varied and interesting.

By moving some of my subject partially off the page, I imply a depth beyond the picture surface.

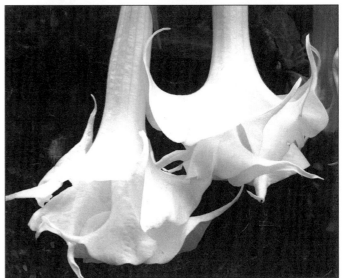

To create better control over where my paint flows, I use a large flat brush and pre-wet the surface in a random way.

** This helps to maintain my white paper, keeping my painting crisp and clean.

**Remember, WATER is the VEHICLE and paint will travel only where that water is placed.

** I use a clean damp brush to tease the paint, which can get stuck against the splashes of masking fluid.

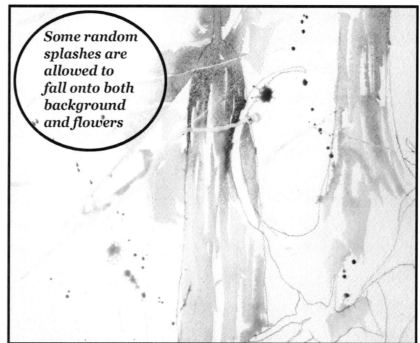

I am constantly aware of placing a light against a dark for impact

If you want a painting to look clean and create impact, VALUE contrasts will help.

For instance, I always try to place a darker value against a light value, and vice versa.

Hence, my work will provide a clearer understanding for my viewer.

I try to use at least three values in my paintings, including the white of the paper.

** Don't forget the middle transitional values. They help ease the eye into the darker values.

I paint the second flower now and begin to use negative painting to bring outside edges into focus.

With the addition of my neat Cobalt Blue and a slightly darker mix of Permanent Sap Green and French Ultramarine Blue, I add some drama.

I float the paint gently, guiding it downwards with clean water to the lower areas of my main flower.

I use a general mix of my original colors for continuity, adding a touch of light Turquoise as well.

** Note the white of the paper is still visible throughout.

I use a thirsty flat brush to lift some areas to imply more ghost-like flowers.

Once I lift out what I need, I dry and reinforce with negative painting.

I concentrate on extending my ghost-like flowers to the lower areas of my painting and underlap them with the front, dominant flowers.

This shows the movement of my design.
I use a zigzag placement of my elements for movement often.
I felt I still needed another ghost-like flower shape, to extend to the bottom of the painting.

After placing my lower ghost flower at the base of my painting to complete my design, I finished off with a little negative painting and dry.

I then remove all masking fluid. A few touch-up areas are needed and I'm done!

The finished painting

Bell Bottom Blues
14" x 20"

Let's Play With Design

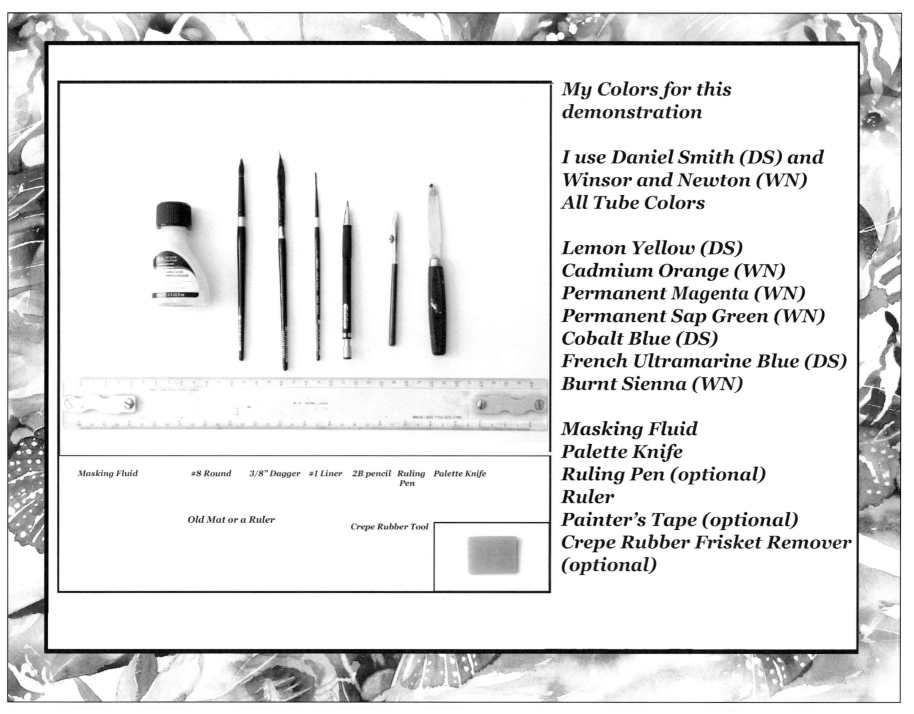

My Colors for this demonstration

I use Daniel Smith (DS) and Winsor and Newton (WN) All Tube Colors

Lemon Yellow (DS)
Cadmium Orange (WN)
Permanent Magenta (WN)
Permanent Sap Green (WN)
Cobalt Blue (DS)
French Ultramarine Blue (DS)
Burnt Sienna (WN)

Masking Fluid
Palette Knife
Ruling Pen (optional)
Ruler
Painter's Tape (optional)
Crepe Rubber Frisket Remover (optional)

Masking Fluid   #8 Round   3/8" Dagger   #1 Liner   2B pencil   Ruling Pen   Palette Knife

Old Mat or a Ruler

Crepe Rubber Tool

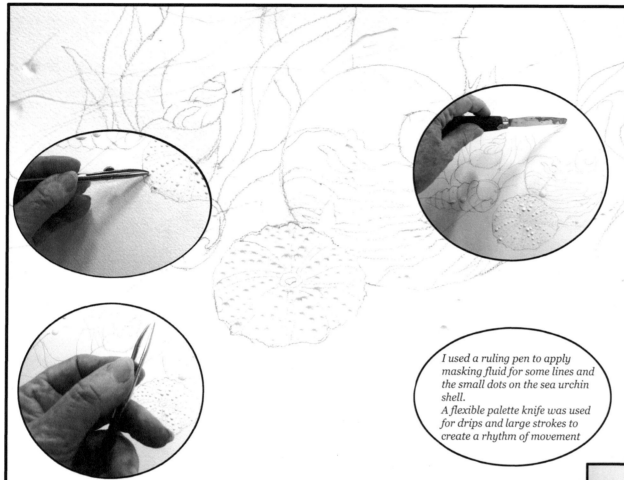

Get to know your tools.

I first drew out my shells and seaweed. I overlap my shapes for depth, placing my subject mostly in the center of the format.

I use a ruling pen and masking fluid to apply some small dots and fine lines on my urchin shell.

** In using a ruling pen, the wider you have the opening, the larger the mark you make. It takes a little practice.

I used a ruling pen to apply masking fluid for some lines and the small dots on the sea urchin shell.
A flexible palette knife was used for drips and large strokes to create a rhythm of movement

A palette knife line of masking fluid is introduced over the background. I include a random splatter over my shells and seaweed to help with the movement I want to portray, echoing an underwater scene.

I then dry the masking fluid and I am now ready to paint.

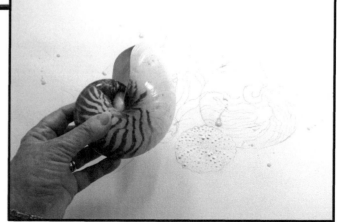

One by one, I paint my shells, always leaving breathing spaces of the white paper showing.

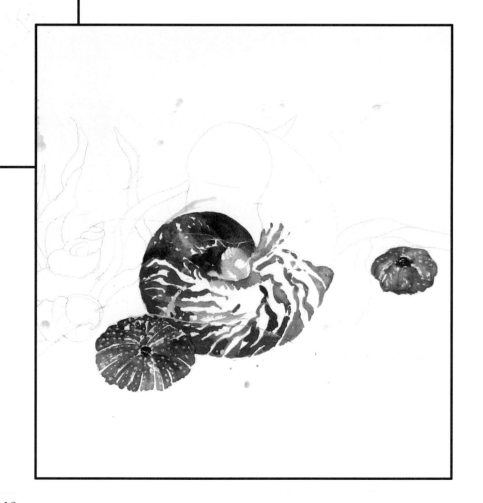

My seaweed is now painted using a mix of Cobalt Blue with my Lemon Yellow.

I am now ready for the geometry design.

This is not something I can really teach you as it's totally intuitive to me.
I do remind you that the geometry's purpose is to guide the eye to the main area of attention.
In this painting, that area is my nautilus shell.

To help with your geometry line, try placing some tracing paper over your painting. Draw your lines on it first as a guide before actually ruling pencil lines on the watercolor paper.

Look at the negative shapes that the geometry makes. Determine that there is a variety of sizes to make the painting interesting.

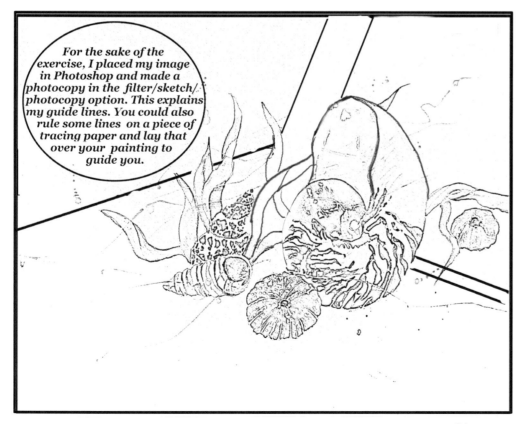

For the sake of the exercise, I placed my image in Photoshop and made a photocopy in the filter/sketch/ photocopy option. This explains my guide lines. You could also rule some lines on a piece of tracing paper and lay that over your painting to guide you.

** I also make sure to break parts of my subject in and out of the geometry for impact.

21

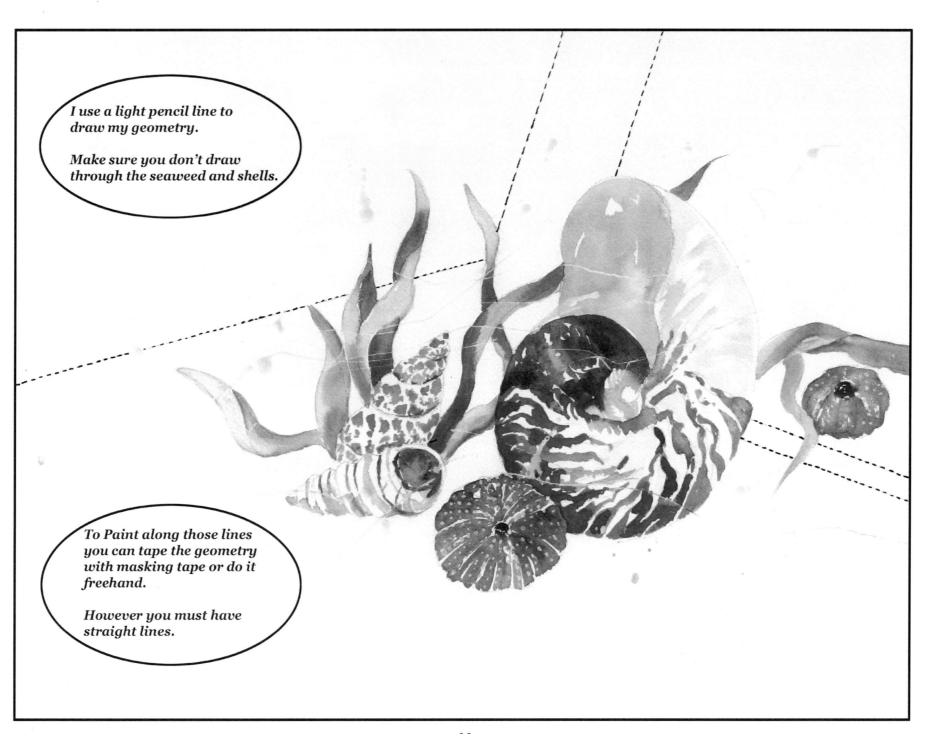

22

I now begin the negative painting.

I use my mix of Cobalt Blue with a touch of French Ultramarine in places.

I weave in and out of the geometry, allowing the subject to be a part of it in places.

I use a little Sap Green, French Ultramarine Blue, and Permanent Magenta to make my very darkest accents.

I am constantly aware of the placement of my values.

Light against dark and vice versa.

I also look at the temperature of my colors, warm against cool and vice versa.

My main objective with my negative painting is to make the geometry and the shells stand out.

I imply some negative spaces in the background for even more linear accents, echoing other seaweed

I make a few negative seaweed-like marks within the background as well.

I am very aware of light against dark and vice versa for drama.

I use my dagger brush for the blue seaweed elements, echoing a less defined version of the positive seaweed I painted earlier.

I use negative painting to reinforce the new shell and bubble shapes.
I also leave areas of my white paper visible.

More shell shapes are added in the background. I plan to leave these as ghost shapes with not a lot of detail.

I don't want to make these new shapes compete with the main focus of attention.

With a round, thirsty brush, I lift out some bubbles in places as well.

NOW I ADD A FEW MORE ELEMENTS

I start to add a few background shell shapes for interest.

Additional seaweed-like elements are added now in some areas and also some bubble-like shapes.
I am very aware of where I add these to best create interest.

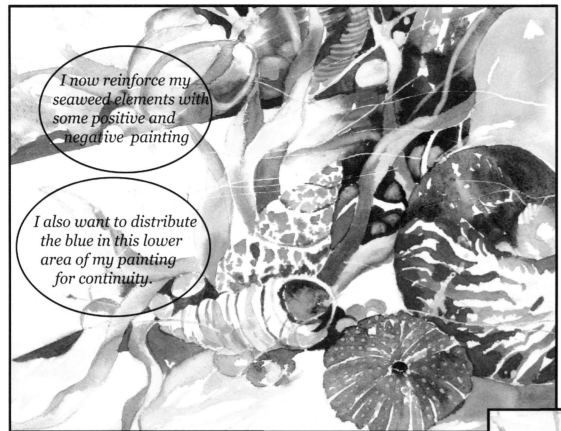

COLOR CONTINUITY is always on my mind.

I feel the blue is such a strong color and decide that a softer version of it, mixed with my green, would be easier on the eye.

It also helps to extend some interest to the left side and lower areas of the composition.

** As a result of these small adjustments, the geometry is now gently focussed in those areas as well.

At this stage, I reinforce some lifted seaweed elements and bubbles to keep everything balanced.

Be careful to distribute the elements throughout. If they are only in one area, they can become too much of a focal point.

** Repeat your elements in different proportions throughout.

** I now thoroughly dry the painting.

I remove the masking fluid with a crepe rubber tool. Using a regular soft white eraser, I remove what pencil marks I can as well.

Time to look at the painting with a critical eye.

I am calling this one done!

Shell Design
14" x 20"

The Drama of Complementary Colors

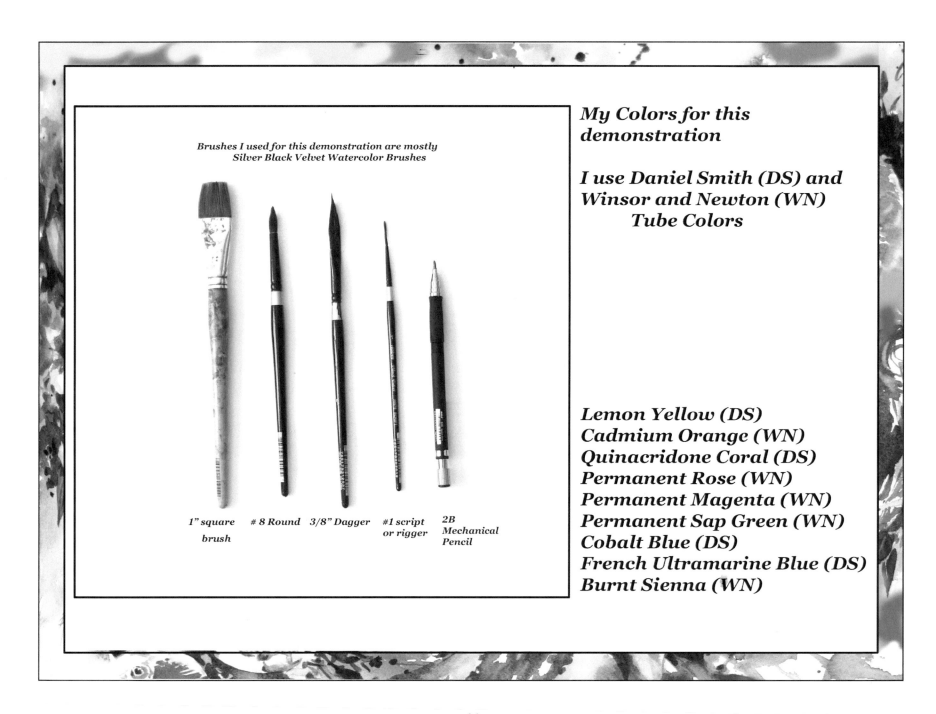

Brushes I used for this demonstration are mostly
Silver Black Velvet Watercolor Brushes

1" square brush   # 8 Round   3/8" Dagger   #1 script or rigger   2B Mechanical Pencil

My Colors for this demonstration

I use Daniel Smith (DS) and Winsor and Newton (WN) Tube Colors

Lemon Yellow (DS)
Cadmium Orange (WN)
Quinacridone Coral (DS)
Permanent Rose (WN)
Permanent Magenta (WN)
Permanent Sap Green (WN)
Cobalt Blue (DS)
French Ultramarine Blue (DS)
Burnt Sienna (WN)

I first draw out my Galah parrots.

** I turn the birds to face each other. This creates TENSION in my subject.

** I combine two different photos using my iPad app (SKETCH CLUB); even doctoring a tree trunk as a perch for the bird on the right.

** My background will be entirely made up.

I am working on Arches Cold Press paper #140. This is my paper of choice for all my book demos.

I begin with the head area. I leave a lot of the white paper visible and just do touches of color at the back of the head for starters. I use a mix of Cadmium Orange, Permanent Magenta, and Quinacridone Coral, and gradually, piece by piece, I work down the bird.

I leave white paper showing to give some breaks within the body, working some different values into the colors to give form to the bird.

I take care to leave some of the white of my paper showing to imply ruffled feathers around the beak and thoughout the body of the bird

For my grays, I use a mix of Cobalt Blue, Permanent Rose, and a touch of Burnt Sienna.

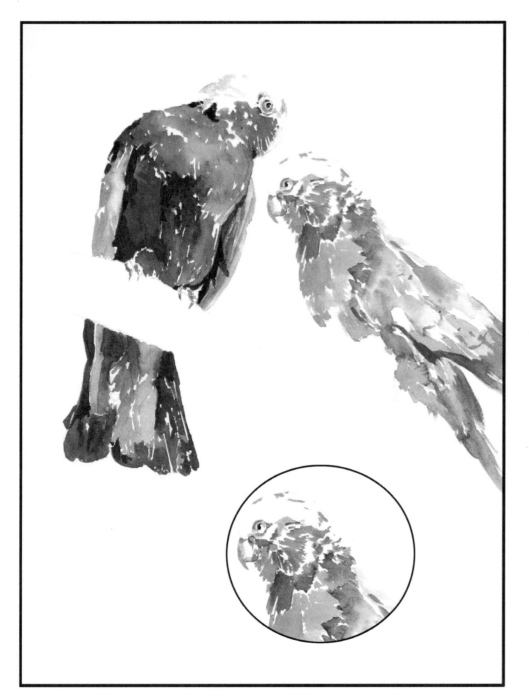

Now for the right-hand bird.

Once again, I leave small linear breaks of the white paper showing through occasionally. This helps with the feather divisions.

** That white paper is your friend.

I also paint the eyes now.

Be careful not to outline the eyes with a continual line. It will look false. Broken lines are best and I use a soft gray with a touch of pink to do this.

I paint the irises of the birds with a mix of Quinacridone Coral and Cadmium Orange.

For the pupils, I use Burnt Sienna and Cobalt Blue.

In beginning the background, I am aware of my placement of values for impact, especially around the heads of the birds.

For the background, I use my round and dagger brushes to ease colors carefully around the heads.

This way, the heads will stand out against the lemon and green mixtures.

** I don't pre-wet my background to paint. I use a wet-into-dry technique, painting a small area first, gently moving the paint away with clean water. I keep adding and joining small controllable areas to this, spreading the paint and enable value changes in this area.

** I use Lemon Yellow, Sap Green, and Cobalt Blue for my background and still leave some white paper showing.

Isolating the tree branches, I flick more of my background colors into the lower part of my painting.

I see areas where I have become too heavy with the darks. I definitely will need to lift some paint to soften these areas and/or camouflage them with foliage.

I see areas I will need to lift out some darks and camouflage with leaves later.

The branches are now painted.

I use a mix of Cadmium Orange and Burnt Sienna for this.

While that is still wet, I add some Burnt Sienna and Cobalt Blue.

I leave the white of the paper showing in places as well.

Far Right...

With my rigger brush, I delineate with a few textural marks.

I use a thirsty brush to lift a few details on the second branch for form.

I work the second branch in much the same way as the first. I don't want to extend this branch down too far. I decide, instead, to just have it 'lost' in the background.

I lift a few lights back into the paint with a thirsty brush.

I lift some leaves with a damp brush

It's now time to try and correct my earlier mistake on the left wing of the left-hand bird. I went way too dark in that area, leaving a line of demarcation between the wing and the chest of the bird.

I soften that inside edge of the wing with a square thirsty brush, then begin lifting out some leaf shapes.

As the new ghost leaves are a new element, I have to place a few throughout the composition for continuity.

I think I have successfully camouflaged the troubling areas with this lifting out technique.

I lightly paint the new leaves and add some positive blue leaves to nestle in amongst them.

I use Cobalt Blue for this.

I adjust some areas of the leaves with cast shadows.

** Note the interplay of those gorgeous complementary colors.

Chat Time 14" x 20"

My painting is finished!

Building Your
Painting In Sections

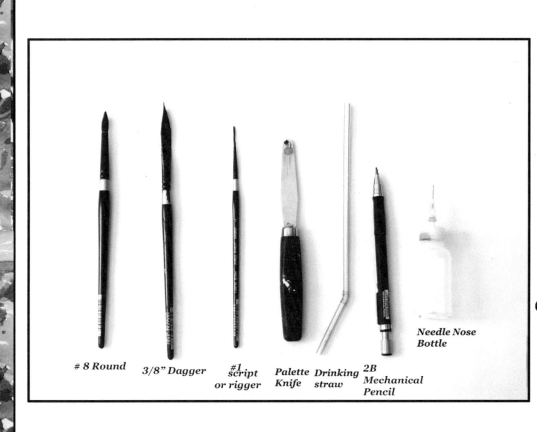

My Colors for this demonstration

I use Daniel Smith (DS) and Winsor and Newton (WN) All Tube Colors

** a small fine metal tipped bottle (also called an oiler) or a Palette knife is fine also
**Drinking Straw

Cadmium Medium Yellow (WN)
Lemon Yellow (DS)
Cadmium Orange (WN)
Aussie Red Gold (DS)
Permanent Rose (WN)
Permanent Magenta (WN)
Permanent Sap Green (WN)
Cobalt Blue (DS)
French Ultramarine Blue (DS)
Burnt Sienna (WN)

 # 8 Round   *3/8" Dagger*   *#1 script or rigger*   *Palette Knife*   *Drinking straw*   *2B Mechanical Pencil*   *Needle Nose Bottle*

After drawing my image on my dry Arches #140 Cold Press paper, I use my dagger brush to paint my foliage colors on the right-hand side of the painting.

I usually begin a landscape with my largest masses.

I always start with a light bright color; in this case, it was Permanent Rose with mixes of both Lemon Yellow, Cadmium Medium Yellow, and Permanent Sap Green.

I am careful of the flow; leaving areas of the white paper still visible to avoid 'muddy' colors.

I spread color with a clean damp brush to get some variation in value.

By building foliage one behind the other I develop depth.

Now for the fun!

I carefully blow edges of my wet paint with my drinking straw.

Don't blow too forcefully with the straw. Short and guided straw marks are easier to control.

42

Using a mix of Aussie Red Gold and Burnt Sienna, I begin to paint the garden wall behind the foliage.

I add to this mixture a combination of Cobalt Blue and Burnt Sienna for shadowed areas.

Using my dagger brush, I start on the wall and foliage on the left of my gate. I treat the whole scene like the pieces of a jigsaw puzzle. This way, I can keep my painting clean and fresh.

I move to the left side of my painting and treat my foliage and wall in the same manner.

I don't use the drinking straw on the left side.

I begin to paint the wall now; starting with a light mix of Aussie Red Gold and then adding Burnt Sienna and Cobalt Blue to weave in and around the foliage.

43

My gate comes next.

I add my background grass.

Using negative painting, I establish the slats of the gate, some distant grass, and a treeline.

** I might mention, I use a very deliberate wet-into-dry technique for most of my painting. I don't pre-wet the surface.

I now begin the foliage behind my fence.

To keep with color continuity, I add a few of the mauve colors used in the right hand foliage areas.

Keeping the values very light at this stage, I use a mix of Cobalt Blue and Permanent Rose here.

Sap Green and Lemon Yellow are added to this mix, tying it all together.

I've established my background now, leaving the tree trunks out.

My colors are cooled down with Cobalt Blue/Sap Green mixes, with a touch of the Permanent Rose/Cobalt Blue as well.

My foreground palette is now linked with my background.

** Remember, yellow is not a good perspective color. It does not recede to give the illusion of distance.

** Never use a strong yellow in your backgrounds. Instead, cool it down and make it less important than your foreground yellows.

Now for the tree trunks.

Having finally decided where my light is coming from, and using my round brush, I begin with Cadmium Orange on the shadow side of the foreground tree. I add to this a little Burnt Sienna with a touch of Cobalt Blue.

I just show peeps of the trees in amongst the foliage I painted earlier.

With a cooler mix of colors, I establish the larger tree trunk behind the wall.

I introduce some Burnt Sienna and French Ultramarine on the shadow side of this trunk.

I use my palette knife to extend and scrap wet paint, making my secondary branches.

Using a light mix of **Permanent Rose and Cobalt Blue,** I place a few shadows on the white gate.

My light source is now more easily determined as coming from the left.

** Remember the eye follows line, and the lines of the pavers are a perfect way to lead your viewer into your painting.

I use my needle nose plastic squirt bottle (also called an oiler), with a small amount of *Aussie Red Gold* in it to make my random lines.

I add a little *Burnt Sienna and Cobalt Blue* to these lines in places as well.

** Take care not to have a line going into a corner.

When dry, I extend my shadows on the path using my dagger brush.

I am at that stage where darks must be adjusted.

I add to my foliage around the foreground tree.

A few darker shadows on the gate itself are needed as well as on my path.

I augment the frontal foliage of my foreground tree.

I use varying hues of my Cobalt Blue and Sap Green mixes, some cooler than others.

I also place foliage behind the wall. This establishes depth.

My distant trees are now in place and I cast some shadows on the lawn for stability.

Garden Gate 14" x 20"

I am calling GARDEN GATE done!

I get asked this question all the time, "How does the artist know the work is complete?"

I think generally if you find yourself fiddling and trying too hard to explain the work, you are at a dangerous point of overworking the painting.

STOP! Take a break, place a mat around it, leave the studio and walk back in to get a fresh glance.

My checklist is as follows:
1. *What attracted me to this scene in the first place?*
2. *Have I portrayed that to my viewer?*
3. *Have I kept the colors clean and left some passageways of white paper showing?*
4. *Do my colors and values read, giving the correct depth of field?*

Working From The Background Forward

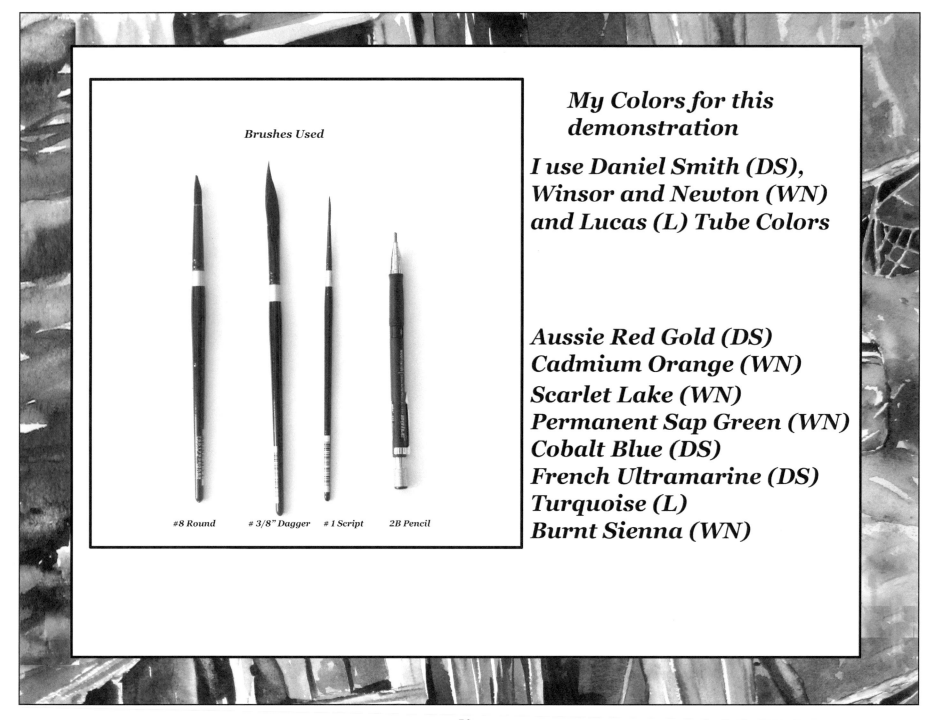

Brushes Used

#8 Round   # 3/8" Dagger   # 1 Script   2B Pencil

My Colors for this demonstration

I use Daniel Smith (DS), Winsor and Newton (WN) and Lucas (L) Tube Colors

Aussie Red Gold (DS)
Cadmium Orange (WN)
Scarlet Lake (WN)
Permanent Sap Green (WN)
Cobalt Blue (DS)
French Ultramarine (DS)
Turquoise (L)
Burnt Sienna (WN)

These are my reference photos off Pixabay.
I plan on painting a composite of these photos.

My main focal point is all about the chickens
themselves. The Shed (or part of it) is only a
backdrop.

I also will make up a few items in the background
as I go.

In this exercise, I plan to work from the background forward.

I first drew out my shed, the chicken, and my rooster.

The positioning of my chickens is important, so I place them facing each other for tension.

I also want the darks of the shed to become a stage for the birds, pushing them forward into the foreground for drama.

I use a mixture of Aussie Red Gold, Burnt Sienna with French Ultramarine Blue in the opening of the shed.

I also imply a few random items in the opening as I paint. These will be enhanced later. I feel it's better than just having a black hole there.

At this time, I begin some negative painting to imply some wire meshing and a trash bin outside the shed.

55

Moving further to the left, I get my shed colors in place.

An occasional line or two with my rigger brush helps define the slats of the wood.

My colors are a mix of Aussie Red Gold and Burnt Sienna. I add French Ultramarine Blue with Scarlet Lake and some streaks of Turquoise.

Notice how that Turquoise color directs the eye to the rooster's head. That's intentional.

In the window opening and the background, I use Permanent Sap Green with a touch of Aussie Red Gold and Lemon Yellow; making it less acidic and to help it recede.

** Remember that yellow is not a perspective color. In 'dirtying' the intensity of that color in my background, it is not commanding too much attention.

I continue further to the left of the shed now, showing a slight roofline for interest.

Nothing has to be too refined. I really want all the interest to be around the chickens.

I can now use a thirsty brush to lift out areas within the opening of the shed, making a broom, a sack and a wheel, just for interest.

** Note the lean of these objects is opposite to the actual lean of the shed. That is intentional.

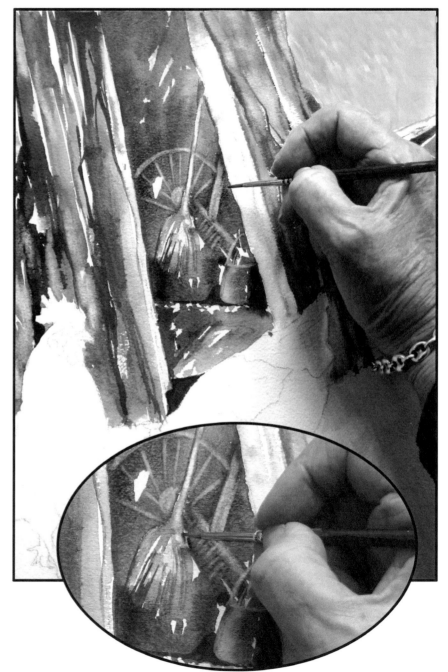

Piece by piece, I get the features started on the chickens.

I used Scarlet Lake with a touch of Cadmium Orange for the combs.

** I add a little gray into the rooster's feathers using a mix of Cobalt Blue and Cadmium Orange.

Now for painting my hen.

I use Scarlet Lake with Aussie Red Gold and a touch of Cadmium Orange on her body.

Burnt Sienna and French Ultramarine Blue are used for my shadow colors on her.

For her feet, I use a light mix of Scarlet Lake and Cobalt Blue.

At this stage, I also paint the trash bin. I used French Ultramarine and some light gray mixes.

For my grays, I use a mix of Cobalt Blue and Cadmium Orange.

** I always mix my grays. It makes them cleaner and fresher than tube grays.

Using negative painting, I add some darks within the opening of the shed and behind the hen.

Again, I especially want the background separated from the birds.

** With some careful adjustment to my values, the eye is able to focus more on my subject.

My rooster is basically white with shadows and a little warmth on some feathers, however not a lot.

I am very aware of light against dark. In refining the rooster's feathers, I also nudge the surrounding darks of the shed to really make him 'pop'.

My painting so far.

Now for the rocks and cast shadows for the chickens.

Using my round brush, I loosely paint my rocks on the left-hand side of the painting.

All my existing grays and earth colors in the painting so far are used in the rocks. I also nudge the background values behind the rocks.

*** Some slightly stronger edges within the rocks are also painted at this stage.*

I use a little Scarlet Lake and Cobalt Blue mix for the cast shadows beneath the chickens.

62

Using my dagger brush loaded with Cadmium Orange and Scarlet Lake, I flick some drops of paint into the lower foreground areas.

At the same time, I use an old toothbrush to spatter some Cadmium Orange in places for a variety of smaller spatter marks.

** I twist my wrist around to get a different direction of spatters.

** I feel this method of a loose spatter includes my foreground without detracting from the subject, and still retains the white of my paper.

Using some torn colored pieces of paper, I place various color values where I think I might need to augment my painting.

This is a great way to assess before you go ahead and paint, possibly ruining your masterpiece.

**Darks behind the hen will help her to 'pop' more.

** I also think the green background is a little flat, so I need to add a change of value there for contrast.

** Just by placing the blue paper in the area where shadows are needed leading to the hen, actually guides me before I start painting.

I can now safely paint my cast shadows to draw the eye towards my hen.

I am calling this on done!

Chicken Coop
12" x 16"

Reflections and
Creating Distance

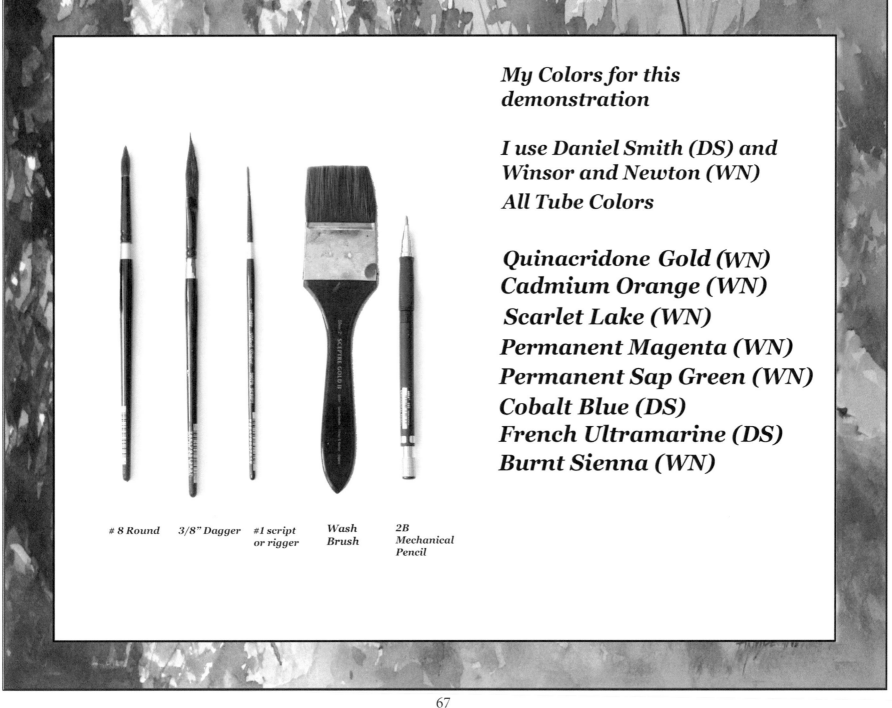

My Colors for this demonstration

I use Daniel Smith (DS) and Winsor and Newton (WN) All Tube Colors

Quinacridone Gold (WN)
Cadmium Orange (WN)
Scarlet Lake (WN)
Permanent Magenta (WN)
Permanent Sap Green (WN)
Cobalt Blue (DS)
French Ultramarine (DS)
Burnt Sienna (WN)

8 Round   3/8" Dagger   #1 script or rigger   Wash Brush   2B Mechanical Pencil

After drawing a rough guide on my Arches #140 Cold Press paper, I begin with my foliage and light colors first. In this case, it's a little Lemon Yellow with Permanent Sap Green and some Cobalt Blue.

**I am using my Dagger Brush for this.

I move across the back line of foliage now. I add Quinacridone Gold to my green and marginally dull down the acidic Lemon Yellow.

With some Cobalt Blue, I add the background sky shape before moving to the frontal foliage at the left of my painting.

This area of foliage is a mixture of Permanent Magenta and both blues. Touches of Sap Green are also added.

I get the back line of water started. I use a thirsty brush to remove some pigment for the softer values.

I begin with soft values on the line of rocks, making sure to leave some white paper visible.

Continuing with the rocks, I add occasional darks among the softer values. No detail.

Now for the water.

I use a wet into wet technique for this.

I tilt my board slightly to allow for gravity to make the paint flow.

I pre-wet the water area with a wash brush; I am ready to paint.

I use my dagger brush to apply my color mixes of Quinacridone Gold, Sap Green, and a touch of Lemon Yellow.

I add a little Cadmium Orange and Scarlet Lake in places as well.

While my paint is wet, I use a flat, thirsty brush to remove a few ripples in the water.

The foliage on the left is now enhanced with some slightly deeper values of Permanent Magenta, Cobalt Blue and a touch of Sap Green.

At this stage, I also add some stronger values in my middle distance treeline along with a few tree trunks.

Millpond
7" x 20"

I added a few final darks in the water, still allowing that passageway of light through to the background.

Middle Distance Treeline...
Quinacridone Gold, Sap Green, Lemon Yellow, Cadmium Orange, Cobalt Blue, French Ultramarine Blue and Burnt Sienna.

Background Sky and Water...
Lemon Yellow, Cobalt Blue and Sap Green.

Rock...
Cobalt Blue, Scarlet Lake, Burnt Sienna and Cadmium Orange.

Left-hand trees...
Permanent Magenta, Sap Green, French Ultramarine Blue and Cobalt Blue.

Water...
Quinacridone Gold, Cadmium Orange, Sap Green, Cobalt Blue and French Ultramarine Blue.

Rocks And Still Water

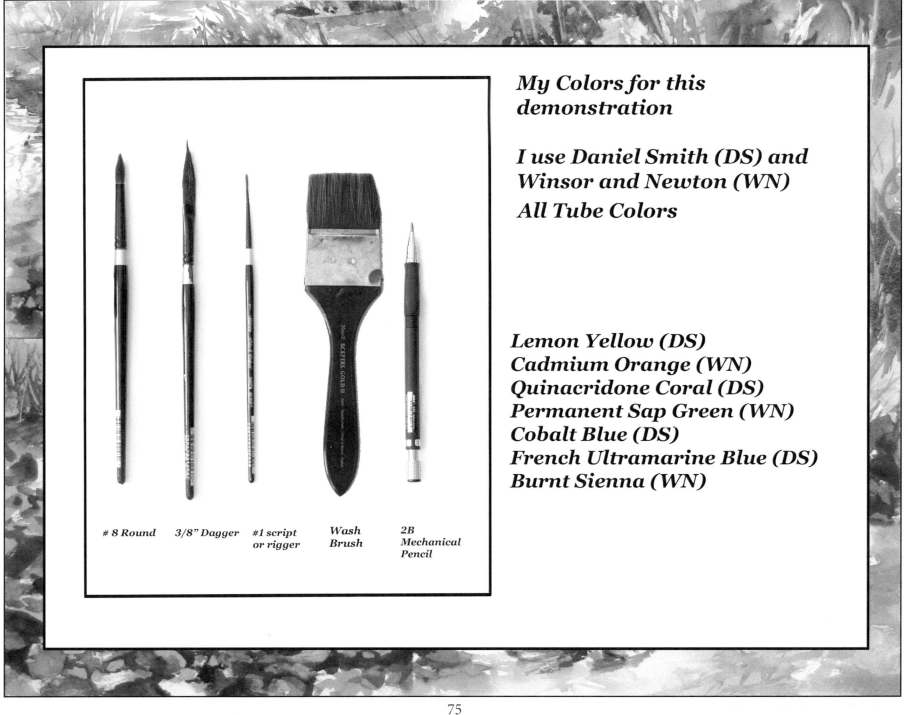

My Colors for this demonstration

I use Daniel Smith (DS) and Winsor and Newton (WN)

All Tube Colors

Lemon Yellow (DS)
Cadmium Orange (WN)
Quinacridone Coral (DS)
Permanent Sap Green (WN)
Cobalt Blue (DS)
French Ultramarine Blue (DS)
Burnt Sienna (WN)

8 Round   3/8" Dagger   #1 script or rigger   Wash Brush   2B Mechanical Pencil

I roughly draw out my scene.

I zapped the colors of my reference shot in my Sketch Club app.

I begin with the background treeline.

I now establish the horizon area.

Using a dagger brush, I use mixes of Quinacridone Coral and Cadmium Orange to start the grasses.

I begin to lay in the background water.

Sap Green and Cobalt Blue are now added to the grasses.

Notice the rhythm of my strokes to imply water. I leave a lot of white paper showing through in a zigzag movement.

I set the stage for my rocks with a scattered underpainting of light and broken washes.

I use my round brush to find some rock shapes. I then use a rigger for line detail.

**Just a dot and dash here and there can be enough.

My fine line rigger is used to negatively delineate around some of the shapes.

I can also use a flat, soft brush to lift out shapes if I need to. These are later reinforced with some negative painting.

Top left...

I add some darker values to my grasses on both right and left embankments now.

Bottom left and above...

Additional ripples and some movement is added to my water.

Top right...

I decide I went a little too dark on the left embankment grasses.

I mix a little white gouache with yellow and orange watercolor. Just a touch is needed to correct this area.

Now for a light sky...

Using my dagger brush, I begin floating some Cobalt Blue with French Ultramarine onto the top left corner of my page.

From left to right...
I tilt my board at a slight angle and pre-wet the area with a large wash brush.

I rarely have a flat blue sky. I like to use a damp paper towel and softly remove an indication of diagonal clouds for movement.

Lower right...
At this time, I add a very light wash of the sky colors to my foreground water area.

** I make sure not to cover all my white paper. By just allowing a gentle lead-in of white paper in the water, my viewer is invited to follow the light.

My painting is now finished!

Sun Dipped Lake 16" x 20"

My last touches involved adding some darker negative values in places amongst the reeds on the right.

A touch more blue is added to the foreground water.

And lastly, I add some additional darks on certain rocks for impact.

Colors I used ...

Background Treeline...
Sap Green, Lemon Yellow, Cadmium Orange
and Cobalt Blue.

Grasses...
Cadmium Orange, Quinacridone Coral, Sap
Green and Cobalt Blue.

Rocky Areas and Embankments...
Quinacridone Coral and Cobalt Blue.
Burnt Sienna and Cobalt Blue with some French
Ultramarine Blue for darks.
Quinacridone Coral and Cadmium Orange for
some highlights.

Background Water...
Cobalt Blue and Sap Green.

Sky and Foreground Water...
Cobalt Blue and French Ultramarine Blue.

Create A Framework
Around Your Subject

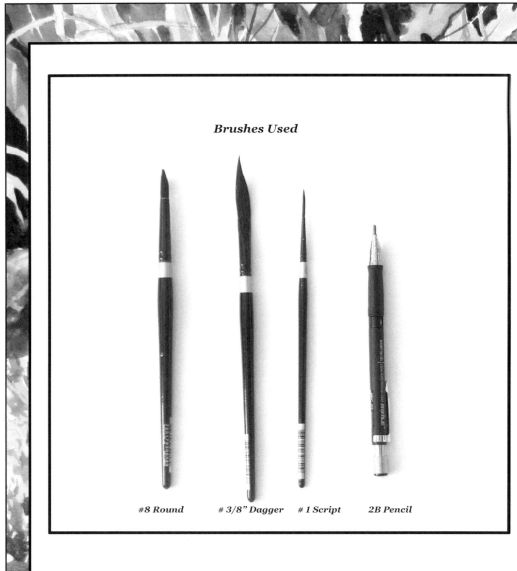

Brushes Used

#8 Round   # 3/8" Dagger   # 1 Script   2B Pencil

My Colors for this demonstration

I use Daniel Smith (DS), Winsor and Newton (WN) and Lucas (L) Tube Colors

Lemon Yellow (DS)
Cadmium Orange (WN)
Quinacridone Coral (DS)
Permanent Rose (WN)
Turquoise (L)
Permanent Sap Green (WN)
Cobalt Blue (DS)
French Ultramarine Blue (DS)
Burnt Sienna (WN)

I begin Rain Forest with a loose drawing of my subject.

I am inspired by the rocks and waterfall of my photo.

However, as with most of my paintings, I use a lot of artistic license during my process.

I paint my colorful leaves first and create a canopy for my waterfall.

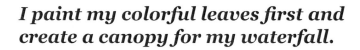

I paint the branch and begin to work across the top area of the painting, section by section.

Little by little, I edge my way across the image. I am always aware of creating interesting, implied textures as I go:

1. Mossy areas on the rocks
2. Some negatively painted branches within darker areas for mystery
3. Some textured, nondistinctive foliage woven into areas

I play the cool against warm colors, as well as vary my tonal values for impact throughout.

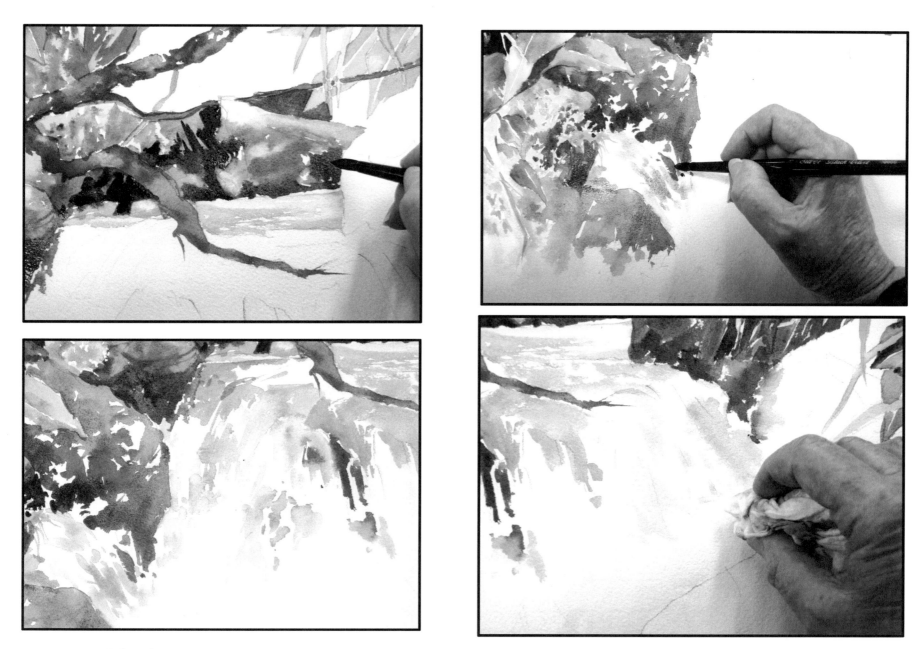

I now tackle the water using my Cobalt Blue/Permanent Rose and soft Sap Green/Cobalt Blue mixes of color. I am careful to leave the white paper showing through. A damp paper towel helps to soften edges of the foam.

88

My painting is coming together now.

I use my dagger brush with some Lemon Yellow and Sap Green for foreground foliage.

I decide that the branch is way too strong. I remove pigment with a thirsty brush and I think it already looks better.

I now add more fernery and distribute some of the blue into my background.

I am getting to the end of this journey.

After adding more of my fern elements in the background, I also distribute that gorgeous Cobalt Blue throughout that area for continuity.

I add a few touches to the water as well and decide on more rocks to peep into the foreground. This helps break all that green.

My last touches are a few more major rocks on the right and a little more random greenery in the bottom right corner.

I also added a few cast shadows over some leaves.

**I set out to feature my waterfall with a frame of foliage.

I think I have achieved my goal.

On to the next project!

Rainforest 16" x 20"

Make A
Bold
Statement

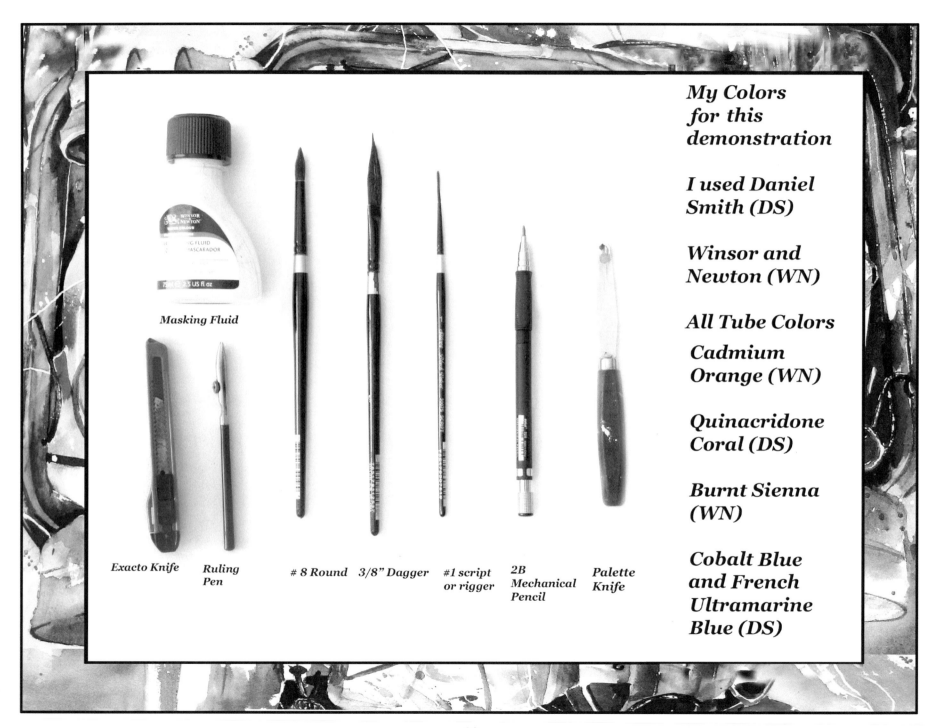

Masking Fluid

Exacto Knife Ruling Pen   # 8 Round   3/8" Dagger   #1 script or rigger   2B Mechanical Pencil   Palette Knife

My Colors for this demonstration

I used Daniel Smith (DS)

Winsor and Newton (WN)

All Tube Colors

Cadmium Orange (WN)

Quinacridone Coral (DS)

Burnt Sienna (WN)

Cobalt Blue and French Ultramarine Blue (DS)

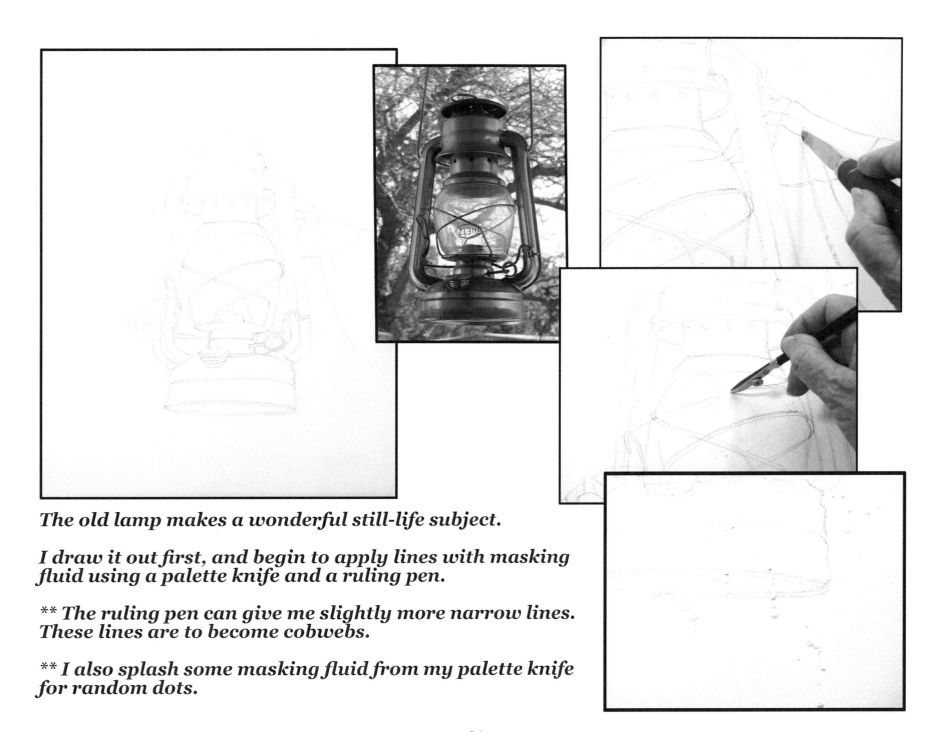

The old lamp makes a wonderful still-life subject.

I draw it out first, and begin to apply lines with masking fluid using a palette knife and a ruling pen.

** The ruling pen can give me slightly more narrow lines. These lines are to become cobwebs.

** I also splash some masking fluid from my palette knife for random dots.

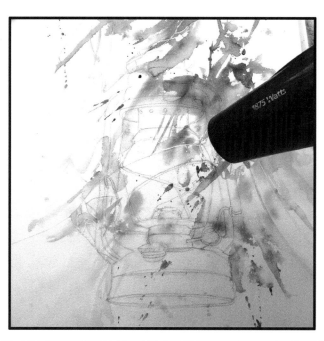

Top left to lower right...

1. I randomly wet my paper with a flat wash brush.

2. Using only Cadmium Orange, I float that color into the wet areas.

3. Now for some Burnt Sienna.

4. Using my dagger brush, I add some Cobalt Blue to my mix.

5) I dry my paper.

I now begin to do some selective negative painting.

** For my darkest darks, I add French Ultramarine Blue to my Burnt Sienna.

** The pure blue areas are Cobalt Blue.

Top Right... I am now adding more detail to my lamp.

** I am very strategic where I augment the darks to best feature my subject.

** In places you will see softer edges and in others, a more refined edge.

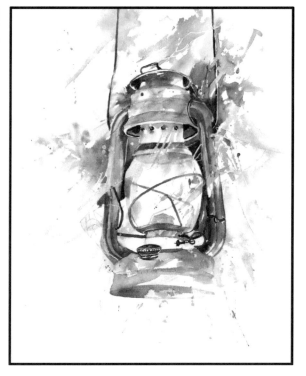

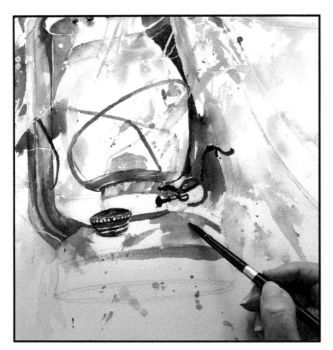

Left...

I now add a small amount of Quinacridone Coral to my Cadmium Orange getting the base of the lamp started.

** I make sure I leave a lot of white paper visible.

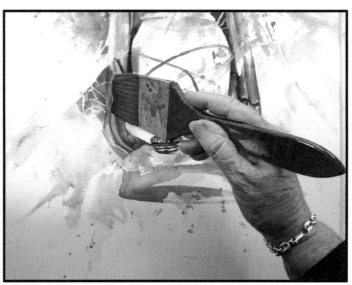

Center Right...

I float some Cobalt Blue into a pre-wetted area at the lower left side of the lamp.

** I want those masking fluid cobwebs to show. A nice zigzag movement is now created with interesting areas of texture and the blue hues.

Far Right...

At this stage, I also add some Burnt Sienna and Cobalt Blue to the lower right outside edge of the lamp. This anchors the subject and helps distribute the blue in that lower third area of the painting.

The unveiling of the masked area is next.
I use my frisket remover for this task.

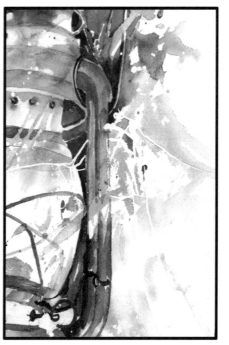

** I like the way some of my cobwebs just disappear into the background.

** I know my cobwebs are too wide in places.

It's especially noticeable in the blue and darker areas.

I will need to use paint to adjust that thickness.

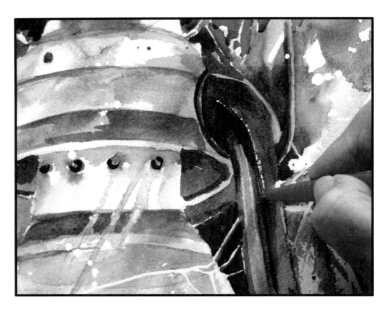

After my paint is all dry, I use an Exacto Knife to chip small, broken lines out of the paper.

** Be aware when you do this not to dig too deeply. You are cutting into the paper after all. If done carefully, this technique is wonderful to get some white sparkle back in places.

My painting is now finished!

This one was great fun to paint.

Memories of Yesteryear
16" x 20"

Overview of the steps and my color choices for this painting.

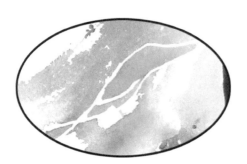

My initial washes were with Cadmium Orange and Burnt Sienna.
** Into that, I added Cobalt Blue.

I am very careful to only pre-wet in a random way to save my white paper. Remember that the water is your vehicle, and the paint will only travel where the page is wet.

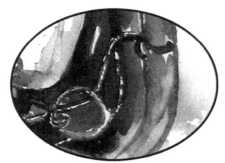

For my darkest darks, I used Burnt Sienna and French Ultramarine Blue.

** For the golden-red glow, I used Quinacridone Coral with Cadmium Orange.

The exacto knife helps to create more fine cobwebs and highlights on the edges of the handle. (Also see above insert.)

Let's Create Textures

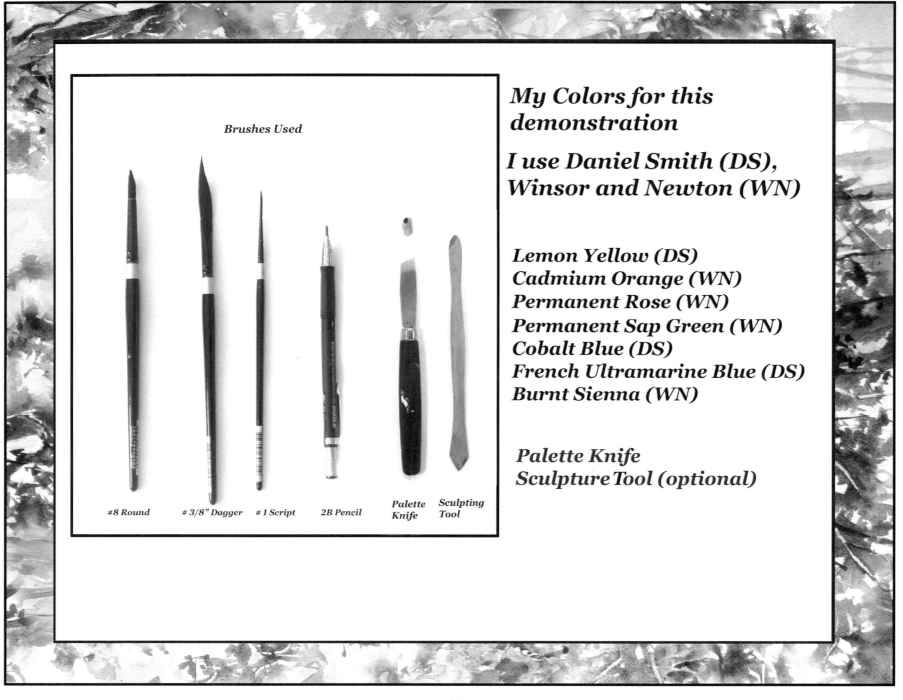

Brushes Used

#8 Round   # 3/8" Dagger   # 1 Script   2B Pencil   Palette Knife   Sculpting Tool

My Colors for this demonstration

I use Daniel Smith (DS), Winsor and Newton (WN)

Lemon Yellow (DS)
Cadmium Orange (WN)
Permanent Rose (WN)
Permanent Sap Green (WN)
Cobalt Blue (DS)
French Ultramarine Blue (DS)
Burnt Sienna (WN)

Palette Knife
Sculpture Tool (optional)

I begin with a faint drawing of my subject, using a photo from which to 'bounce'.

I am taking my own artistic license with the elements as you will see; a photograph, for my purposes, is merely an inspirational beginning.

Using my #8 Round Brush, I begin with Cadmium Orange to which I add some Permanent Rose.

While that is still wet, I add Burnt Sienna with some Cobalt Blue.
*** As with all my paintings, I leave little breaks of the white paper showing through.*

Before my painting completely dries, I use my palette knife for some of the bark textures.

I also use a wooden sculpting tool, which has a rounded end. This tool, (normally used on clay), can scrape some nice soft bark-like textures as well.

** Both these tools can be manipulated to give different marks.

If a sculpture tool, such as I am using, is not available, improvise with an ice cream stick or similar.

** The Palette Knife gives a sharper, fat and thin mark, depending on how much of the knife you use. The wooden tool makes a softer linear mark.

** Learn to try different tools for the marks you make. It will vary your textures. Not all tools have to be actual art tools. Improvise!

Now for the fernery area.

I use a mixture of Lemon Yellow and Permanent Sap Green for this.

While my ferns are drying, I mix my Cobalt Blue with Permanent Rose for that gorgeous mauve color.

** This makes a nice interplay of warm and cool complementary colors.

Some Cobalt Blue is added to my Lime Green, softening the acidic hues.

** I will often play with that contrast of my colors, such as warm against cool and opposite complementary colors on the color wheel.

** This helps stimulate the eye for my viewers.

Still using a wet-into-dry watercolor technique, I begin to establish the back line of trees.

** I have a lot more control over the paint if I don't pre-wet the area.

** As this area is well away from the foreground trees, I can make my colors and values a lot more muted. They are the same colors as I used earlier, however I add more water to dilute them.

** I also don't add any of that texture used in the larger frontal trees.

I add background foliage using Cadmium Orange and Permanent Rose.

Using my dagger brush, I move to the foliage on the front trees now using mixes of Cobalt Blue and Permanent Rose first, then Sap Green and Cobalt Blue.

A few palette knife branches are now made after the foliage paint subsides a little.

Forest Walk. 16" x 20"

I am gradually coming to the completion of Forest Walk.

** With the addition of a few shadows, more fernery on my pathway and some adjustments to my dark textured trunks; I now feel the painting is more 'pulled together'.

** More fine branches are added to my frontal trees. With a thin thirsty brush, I remove a few grass-like lines from that blue/mauve mass.

** I then add a mix of Lime Green watercolor and White Gouache for contrast. This now opens that area a little.

I am calling this one Finished!

The various steps of this painting.

Cadmium Orange and Permanent Rose were the first colors I used on the foreground tree trunks.

I added Burnt Sienna and Cobalt Blue for the darks, and used both a palette knife and a wooden sculpture tool to scrape the linear textures.

I began with Lemon Yellow and Permanent Sap Green for the fernery, and added some Cobalt Blue and Permanent Rose to areas around this.

For my lower foliage and shrubs, I used Cobalt Blue and Permanent Rose.

For the canopy in the foreground tree, I used Lemon Yellow, Cobalt Blue, and some Permanent Sap Green with a little of the mauve mixture.

For my distant trees, I used mixtures of Cadmium Orange and Cobalt Blue with a touch of Permanent Rose.

I later added a touch of Burnt Sienna and Cobalt Blue to my two larger distant trees on the left.

Rae's Tips and Pearls of Wisdom

1) Remember that curvilinear lines are gentler to ease the eye through your composition.

2) I use a zigzag or 'S' shape on which to place elements throughout my works. This can be an actual broken path, or even by using strategically placed colors, values, other elements or shapes. These additions allow the viewer's eye to 'bounce' through your painting visually.

3) Remember to vary the values and intensity of your colors. I try to have at least 3 values including the white of the paper.

4) Keep your painting fresh. Don't lose that white paper. If you wet the whole page first, you are in danger of deadening your masterpiece with too much color.
** Therefore, I advise you to only dampen the paper in random areas. The paint will basically travel where the paper is wet, enabling more control over it.

5) The first pass is the easiest. It's the second pass which can trip you up. People tend to go too dark too soon.
** Before jumping into the darks, remember the middle and transitional values as well.

6) Any lines will guide the eye. I will often use line strategically, to guide my viewer to the focus of attention.
** This is also where broken, curved line work better than straight diagnals.

7) *Objects placed in a line can also create direction. A row of houses, trees or fence posts will create a line. Even areas of color, if placed in a row, will attract attention and the viewer will mentally form a line.*

8) *Remember, in ART, the term 'BALANCE' is actually 'IMBALANCE'. Think of a see-saw with an adult on one end and a child on the other. Use that weight distribution in your painting.*
The larger of the objects will be the main focus. The smaller ones will be less important.
They merely 'balance' and enhance the focal point.

9) *In the same respect as the above tip, be careful not to SPLIT YOU 'COMPOSITION'. If the space in between your focus and secondary or even teriary focus is too even, there might be a problem. You could end up with 2 or 3 paintings, each area claiming the main attention.*

10) *Paint your large masses first. Work out how to balance that mass with smaller, less important masses.*

11) *When painting a landscape, I like to get my larger areas painted first. However, I will often leave the sky unpainted and make my final decisions on that till the end of my painting.*

12) *Alternatively, if my painting is basically a SKYSCAPE and is all about that area, I will pre-wet the sky and begin there as my strategy.*

13) I'm a colorist by heart and this means I use color to create the mood in my paintings. For instance the cooler blues, greens and mauves evoke a more relaxed response. A warmer set of colors will awaken the senses and create energy and drama.

** With this color psychology in mind, decide your painting's purpose before you begin, and choose your palette accordingly.

14) I usually begin in the area I want as the main focus of attention.
** However that is just a starting point, not to be labored on too long and in danger of becoming overworked. Work the other areas of the painting as well, and keep the balance of attention active. (see-saw)

15) I am mostly a studio painter. However, the experience for artists to work outdoors is very rewarding. It enables the artist to work fast and places less importance on the embellishments, instead capturing the fleeting feeling of light seen at first glance.
** Ask yourself what attracted you to this scene in the first place? That's what you as the AUTHOR must portray to your READER.
** Was it the light, a certain shape, the drama of values or maybe color? All of these elements in your painting will help the reader better understand your motivation.

16) Don't get stuck in a rut. Vary your subject matter. It's very easy to get comfortable just painting a genre you have mastered. However, it's exciting to challenge oneself and step outside of the 'box' occasionally.

Above all, grow your skills and have fun!

Rae's Gallery Pages

Rae conducts online Zoom lessons in her Dancing Brushes Club.

If interested, please contact her through her website: raeandrews.com

Prints of Rae's work are available at: Fine Art America.

CPSIA information can be obtained
at www.ICGtesting.com
Printed in the USA
LVRC082331240821
696051LV00003B/91